Light and Sound

KINGFISHER

a Houghton Mifflin Company imprint
222 Berkeley Street
Boston, Massachusetts 02116
www.houghtonmifflinbooks.com

First published in 2007
2 4 6 8 10 9 7 5 3 1
1TR/1106/PROSP/RNB/140MA/F

LIBRARY OF CONGRESS CATALOGING-IN-PUBLICATION DATA
Goldsmith, Michael.
Light and sound/Mike Goldsmith. —1st ed.
p. cm. — (Kingfisher young knowledge)
Includes index.
ISBN-13: 978-0-7534-6036-8
1. Light—Juvenile literature. 2. Sound—Juvenile literature. I. Title.
QC360.G655 2007
535—dc22
2006022387

Senior editor: Belinda Weber
Coordinating editor: Stephanie Pliakas
Designer: Rebecca Johns
Cover designer: Poppy Jenkins
Picture research manager: Cee Weston-Baker
DTP coordinator: Catherine Hibbert
DTP operator: Claire Cessford
Production controller: Jessamy Oldfield
Indexer: Hilary Bird

ISBN 978-0-7534-6036-8

Printed in China

Acknowledgments
The publishers would like to thank the following for permission to reproduce their material. Every care has been taken
to trace copyright holders. However, if there have been unintentional omissions or failure to trace copyright holders,
we apologize and will, if informed, endeavor to make corrections in any future edition.
b = bottom, *c* = center, *l* = left, *t* = top, *r* = right

Pages: *cover* Alamy/Stockbyte; 1 Alamy/Stockbyte; 2–3 Corbis; 4–5 Corbis/Zefa; 6–7 Getty/Stone; 7 Science Photo Library (SPL)/
Larry Landolfi; 8*l* Corbis/Randy Farris; 9*tr* Getty/Stone; 9*bl* Natural History Picture Agency/James Carmichael Jr; 10–11 Alamy/Stock
Connection; 12*c* Corbis/Walter Hodges; 12–13 Corbis/Zefa; 13*t* Nature Picture Library/David Shale; 14 Corbis; 15*t* Getty/Stone;
15*b* SPL; 16 Corbis/Aaron Horowitz; 17*t* SPL/Celestial Image Co.; 17*b* Nature Picture Library/Jorma Luhta; 18–19 Corbis;
19*tl* Alamy/Phototake Inc.; 20 Corbis/RoyMorsch; 21*t* Alamy/Imageshopstop; 21*b* SPL/Lawrence Lawry; 22 Getty/Photographer's Choice; 23*t*
Alamy/Sami Sarkis; 23*b* SPL/NASA; 24 Brand X Pictures; 25*t* Corbis/NASA; 25*b* SPL/Custom Medical Stock Photo; 26 Alamy/Oote Boe; 27*t*
SPL/Merlin Tuttle; 27 SPL; 28 Alamy/A. T. Willett; 28*t* Alamy/Imagestate; 30–31 Alamy/Butch Martin; 31*c* Corbis/Zefa; 32*br*
Getty/Imagebank; 32–33 Corbis/Zefa; 33*t* Getty/Imagebank; 34 Corbis/Bill Ross; 35*bl* Getty/Imagebank; 35*r* Corbis/Carmen Redondo;
36 Frank Lane Picture Agency/David Hosking; 37 Corbis; 37*br* Getty/Photodisc Red; 38 Getty/Johner Images; 39*tl* Alamy/Profimedia; 39*b*
Getty/Photonica; 40*l* Photolibrary.com; 40*r* Corbis; 41*t* SPL/Hank Morgan; 41*b* SPL/NASA; 48 Corbis/Pat Doyle

Illustrations on pages: 8, 30 Sebastien Quigley (Linden Artists); 10, 11 Encompass Graphics
Commissioned photography on pages 42–47 by Andy Crawford Project-maker and photo shoot coordinator: Jane Thomas
Thank you to models Mary Conquest, Darius Caple, Jamie Chang-Leng, and Georgina Page

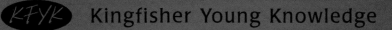

Kingfisher Young Knowledge

Light and Sound

Dr. Mike Goldsmith

KINGFISHER
BOSTON

Contents

World of light

We need light in order to live. It gives us day and night, colors, pictures, stars, and rainbows. We also use it to play CDs and make electricity.

The bright Sun

The Sun is a star. It is a huge ball of burning gas that gives us light and warmth. Without it, there would not be any life on Earth.

gas—a shapeless substance, such as air, that is not solid or liquid

Looking at the stars

Using telescopes, scientists can see even more light from the stars. They can figure out how far away from Earth the stars are, how hot they are, and what they are made of.

telescope—a device that makes things look bigger than they really are

Eyes and seeing

People need light to be able to see. Many nighttime animals can see with less light than we need. They have big eyes, which take in as much light as possible.

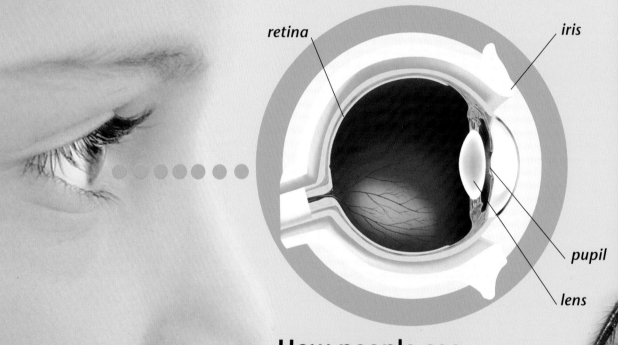

retina

iris

pupil

lens

How people see

Light bounces off objects and into the eye through the pupil. The lens focuses the light on the retina, and the brain figures out what you are seeing.

iris—the colored part of the eye

Animal eyes

Nighttime animals, like this owl, have huge eyes. They can see well in the dark and hunt at night.

eyes

Spider eyes

Spiders are hunters and need to catch insects to eat. Many spiders have eight eyes, and they can see in all directions at once.

retina—*a special layer at the back of the eye that picks up light*

Color

People can see millions of different colors. Colors can be mixed in different ways—every pigment mixed together makes black, and all the colors of light mixed together make white.

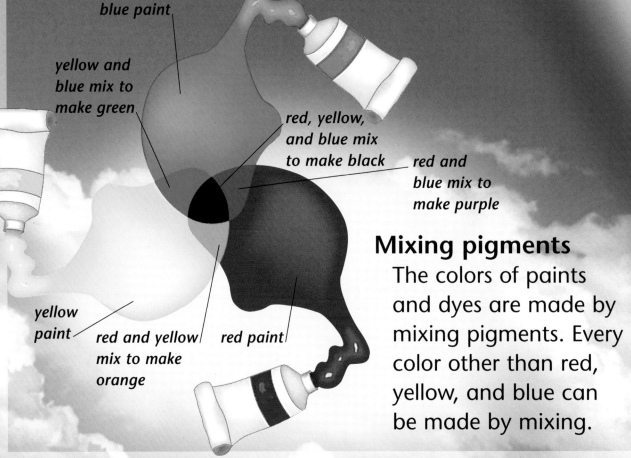

blue paint

yellow and blue mix to make green

red, yellow, and blue mix to make black

red and blue mix to make purple

yellow paint

red and yellow mix to make orange

red paint

Mixing pigments

The colors of paints and dyes are made by mixing pigments. Every color other than red, yellow, and blue can be made by mixing.

pigments—substances that give something its color

green light

red light

all the colors of light mixed together make white

green and red mix to make yellow

blue and green mix to make cyan

blue light

red and blue mix to make magenta

Mixing lights

Lights mix in a different way than pigments do. All colors are made by mixing different amounts of red, blue, and green light.

Separating light

Sunlight (white light) is a mixture of colors. Raindrops separate these colors to make a rainbow of red, orange, yellow, green, blue, indigo, and violet.

separating—splitting apart

Making light

Anything will shine with light if it gets hot enough. Most of the light that we see comes from hot objects—such as the Sun, lightbulbs, and stars.

Electric light

Some substances glow with light when electricity passes through them. When electricity is passed through neon gas, it gives off colored light that can be used in advertising signs.

neon—an invisible gas that glows when electricity passes through it

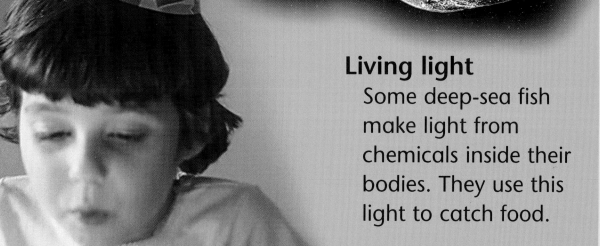

Living light

Some deep-sea fish make light from chemicals inside their bodies. They use this light to catch food.

Birthday lights

Flames give off light as well as heat. The candles on this birthday cake glow brightly as they burn.

chemicals—substances that combine and react with each other

14 Light from the Sun

For billions of years, the Sun's light has shone on our world. It is millions of miles away, yet it is still dangerous to look directly at it.

Life from light

Every living thing on Earth needs sunlight. The leaves of plants trap sunlight in order to grow.

liquid—a runny substance

Glowing sunsets

As Earth spins, the Sun moves across the sky. When the Sun is low in the sky, it looks red because its light passes through the thick, dusty air close to the ground.

Staying warm

Heat from the Sun keeps Earth's oceans liquid. Without the Sun, all the water and air around the planet would be frozen.

land

ocean

frozen—turned into ice

Darkness and light

When there is no light, we see darkness. Our planet spins in space—when it turns away from the Sun, it is nighttime. We need other sources of light in order to see in the dark.

Moonlight
The Moon does not make its own light. Sunlight bounces off it and makes it glow.

source—where something comes from; for example, the Sun is a source of light

Stars

Stars make their own light. Many are brighter than our planet's star, the Sun. Stars look very faint because they are so far away.

Nature's light show

The Sun sends out particles that carry electricity. These can bounce off particles in the air, making the sky glow with different colors.

particles—very small pieces

Shadows

When something blocks light, it casts a shadow. It is cooler and darker in a shadow because shadows are cut off from the Sun's warmth and light.

Shadows

All solid objects cast shadows. They may be long or short, depending on how the sunlight falls on them.

blocks—*gets in the way of*

Darkness by day

Sometimes the Moon passes between Earth and the Sun. It blocks our view of the Sun, causing darkness. This is called a solar eclipse.

solar—*having to do with the Sun*

Bouncing light

Light bounces off most objects. A lot of light bounces off snow, so it shines brightly in sunlight. Coal doesn't let any light bounce off it, so it is dark.

Seeing double

The surface of a mirror is so smooth that it bounces back light in exactly the same pattern as it receives it. This is called a reflection.

reflection—the image of what is in front of a mirror

Bright nights

In this picture, the Sun's light has bounced off the Moon to the sea, making the sea shine with light.

Talking with light

Light can travel through glass threads called optical fibers. These fibers can carry telephone calls and computer signals.

optical fibers—*thin threads of glass along which light can pass*

22 Bending light

Objects that light can travel through are called transparent. When light enters a transparent substance—such as glass or water—it bends.

Funny shapes

When light travels between water and air, it bends and what we see seems out of shape. The bending light has made this boy's body look bigger in the water.

transparent—see-through or clear

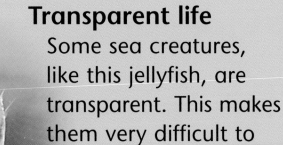

Transparent life

Some sea creatures, like this jellyfish, are transparent. This makes them very difficult to see in the deep and cloudy water.

Bigger and brighter

Magnifying lenses are fatter in the middle. They bend light and make things look bigger than they actually are.

magnifying—*making something seem bigger than it really is*

Electric light

Light can make electricity, and electricity can make light. In a lightbulb, electricity heats up a thin wire so that it glows.

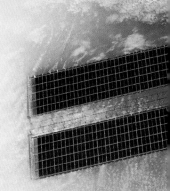

Electric light

By coloring the glass of these lightbulbs, different colored lights are produced. Lightbulbs get hot when they ar turned on, so do not touch them.

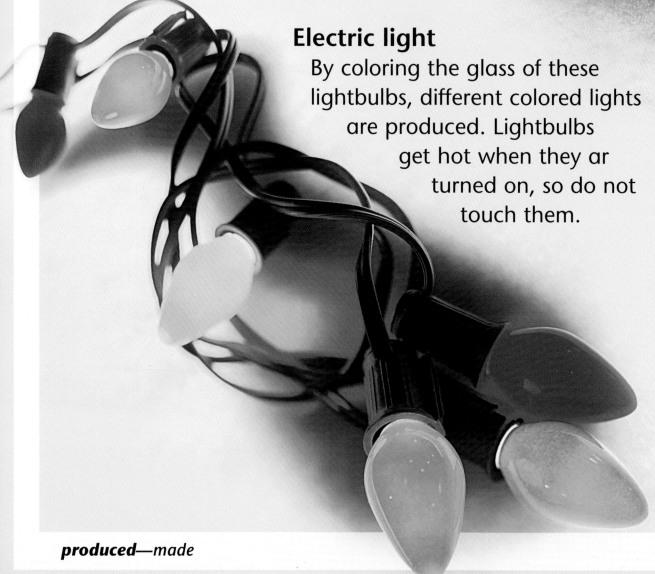

produced—made

Solar power
Solar panels outside this space station collect sunlight and turn it into electricity. The electricity is then used to power things.

Laser surgery
Very narrow beams of light, called lasers, can be used for many things. Lasers are used in delicate operations such as eye surgery.

delicate—needing or using great care

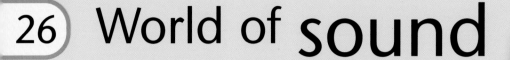

World of sound

There are sounds all around us. We listen to music and hear voices. Sound has many other uses too. It can "draw" pictures and help animals find their prey.

Unwelcome sounds
Sounds that are unpleasant to listen to, such as the sound of heavy drills, are called noise.

unwelcome—*not wanted*

Sounds in the dark

Bats use sound to hunt. They give a shrill call that bounces off any solid object. They hear the echo and figure out where their food is.

Sounds healthy

Doctors use sound to create pictures of unborn babies. Sound waves bounce off the baby, and computers can "draw" the picture.

echo—a sound that bounces off an object

What is sound?

Sound is a type of wave or ripple. Like ripples in a pond, sound travels in every direction. Sounds get quieter the farther you are from their source.

Boom!

Some airplanes travel faster than sound does. They make a shock wave in the air. This can be heard as a loud bang called a sonic boom.

sonic boom—*the noise created when something travels faster than the speed of sour*

Silent space

Sound can travel through air or water. There is no air or water in space, so there is no sound.

Sound speeds

Sound travels quicker through water than through air. These killer whales use clicks and whistles to communicate underwater.

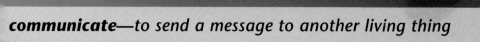

communicate—to send a message to another living thing

How do we hear?

When sound enters the ear, it travels down a tube. The tube's end is covered by a very thin wall of skin called the eardrum.

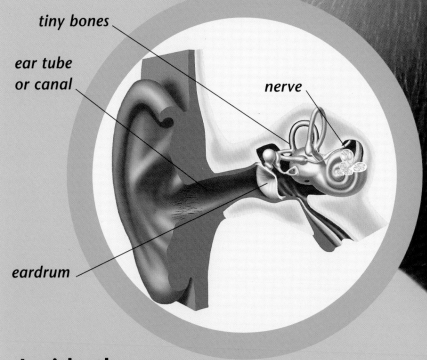

tiny bones

ear tube or canal

nerve

eardrum

Inside the ear

When a sound hits the eardrum, it wobbles and makes the tiny bones inside the ear vibrate.

vibrate—to move rapidly back and forth

Hearing

Nerves in the ear send
messages to the brain.
The brain figures out what
sound is being heard.

Animal ears

Most animals can hear, but not
many have ears like ours. The
fennec, a type of fox, has huge
ears. They can turn around to
pick up very faint sounds.

nerves—special fibers that run from the brain to all parts of the body

Making sound

Sound is usually made when something moves backward and forward very quickly. The moving thing might be a leaf in the breeze, the metal piece inside a bell, or a guitar string.

Musical sounds

Blowing a trumpet makes a buzzing sound in the mouthpiece. This sound travels through the trumpet to make music.

mouthpiece—the part of a musical instrument that goes over or inside the mouth

Voices

When you speak or sing, two flaps of skin in your throat wobble. These are called vocal cords.

Snaps and crackles

Sound can be a burst, like a balloon popping or fireworks exploding. We hear the fireworks' crackles and fizzes while watching the sky.

vocal cords—*flaps of skin that enable humans to speak*

How sound travels

Sounds travel as waves through air, water, or solid objects. The waves eventually die away, but they can travel long distances first.

Long journeys
A busy street is a noisy place. The sounds of people talking, cars, and other vehicles can travel a long way.

vehicles—anything used for moving people or things

Echoes

Sound waves bounce
back from hard objects,
like walls. We call
these sounds echoes.

*the echo bounces
off the cave wall,
and the same shout
is heard again*

child shouts

Quiet or loud?

The more a sound wave wobbles, the louder it sounds. One of the loudest natural sounds is when a volcano erupts. Bombs and rocket engines make the loudest human sounds.

Shhh . . .

Some animals can hear sounds that are too quiet for people. An aardvark can hear termites crawling under the ground.

natural—occurring in nature; not made by people or machines

Ouch!

Very loud sounds can damage your ears. Our ears tense up when they hear loud noises, making everything sound muffled (softer and less clear).

damage—to hurt or cause injury

High or low?

Sound waves wobble at different speeds.
The faster the sound waves wobble,
the higher the sound that they produce.
Sounds that wobble slower are lower.

Making music
Violin strings move quickly
and make a high sound.
Most guitar strings move
more slowly, so their
sound is lower.

produce—to make or create

High meows and low roars

Kittens have small vocal cords and weak lungs, so they make high, quiet meows. Lions are big cats with powerful lungs. They make low, loud roars.

lungs—the parts inside the body that are used for breathing

Electric **sound**

Sound can be changed into electricity. The electricity can then be changed back into sound again. This happens when you talk on the telephone.

Microphones

A microphone changes sound into a wobbling pattern of electricity. A loudspeaker turns these patterns back into sound.

loudspeaker

microphone

loudspeaker—*a device that changes electricity into sound*

Changing sound

By turning sound into pictures like this one, scientists can see what we hear. These pictures are called sonograms.

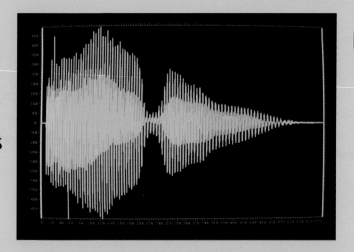

Voices from space

When astronauts are outside a spacecraft, they communicate using microphones and loudspeakers.

sonogram—a computer-generated picture of a sound

Shadow puppets

Make animal puppets

Solid shapes block the light and cast shadows. You can make different shaped shadows, like this dragon, and put on a shadow puppet show.

You will need
- Pencil
- Colored paper
- Scissors
- Candy wrappers
- Tape
- Straws or sticks
- Flashlight

Draw a dragon with a long, pointed tail, feet, and an open mouth onto a piece of colored paper.

Carefully cut out the dragon using scissors. Ask an adult to help you do this.

On one side, tape on candy wrappers to makes flames coming out of the dragon's mouth.

You can make other shadow puppets, like a cat or a bird.

4

Tape a straw or short stick to the back. Turn the dragon over and draw an eye, nose, and wings.

5

In a darkened room, ask a friend to shine a flashlight onto a plain wall. This will make a shadow.

Position your shadow puppet in front of the flashlight and move it around in the light.

Shadow clock

Tell the time by shadows

Shadow clocks measure time by using shadows cast by the Sun. Have fun making your own clock.

1

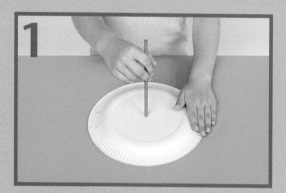

Make a small hole in the middle of a paper plate and stand a straw upright in the hole.

You will need
- Paper plate
- Straw
- Markers

Keep your clock in the same place, and when the shadows fall, you'll be able to tell the time.

2

Put the plate in a sunny place. Every hour, draw a line along the shadow that the straw makes and write down the time.

Xylophone

Make music

You can make a simple xylophone using glasses of water and a wooden spoon.

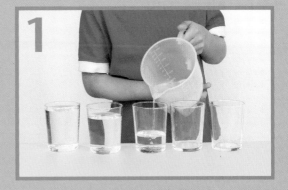

You will need
- 5 glasses, all the same size
- Pitcher of water
- Food coloring
- Wooden spoon

Line up the glasses and pour water into them. Fill the first up to the top and then the rest with a little less water than the one before it.

You can add a few drops of different food coloring to the glasses in order to color the water.

Gently tap each glass with the spoon, and you will hear that each one makes a different sound.

Plastic-cup telephone

Make a working phone

You can make sound travel along a piece of stretched-out string. The plastic cups act like the microphone and the loudspeaker so that you can hear what your friend is saying.

You will need
- 2 plastic cups
- Stickers and colored paper
- Scissors
- Modeling clay
- Sharp pencil
- Piece of string, 15–20 ft. long

1

Decorate two clean, empty plastic cups with stickers and shapes cut out from pieces of colored paper.

The sound of your voice travels along the string.

2

Place a ball of modeling clay underneath each cup and make a hole in the bottom with a sharp pencil.

3

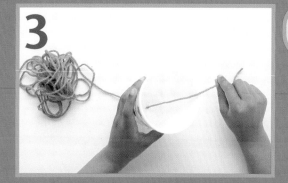

Thread one end of the string through the hole and then tie a knot at the end.

4

Do the same thing with the other cup. Give a friend one cup and stretch out the string. Talk into the cup.

If your friend holds the other cup to his or her ear, he or she will hear what you are saying.

Index